汉语桥-中学生夏令营
Chinese Bridge Summer Camp for Foreign Students

中国欢迎你 Welcome to China 短期汉语系列教材

孔子学院总部/国家汉办
Confucius Institute Headquarters(Hanban)

Xue Jianzhi

学剪纸

Chinese Paper-cuts

修订版 Revised Edition

U1001166

才艺类

高等教育出版社·北京

“中国欢迎你”短期汉语系列教材

总策划 许 琳

总监制 王永利

策 划 陈 默 邵亦鹏

监 制 梁 宇 薛 佼

编委会成员（按姓名音序排列）

常 春	迟兰英	代凝慧	丁 磊	丁 颖	董 赟
范祖奎	冯丽君	郝永宁	贺红梅	侯晓彬	纪仁盛
贾静芳	贾腾飞	姜志琪	金飞飞	鞠 慧	孔庆国
孔雪晴	李红艳	李 娜	梁小岸	梁 云	刘芳珍
刘玉波	卢小燕	罗来莉	罗兴平	孟宪滨	那泽汗
秦晓燕	孙秀杰	屠晓蓓	汪正才	王 岱	王文龙
王 艳	王亦琳	王 瑜	王玉静	温 培	吴玉为
席忠祥	许 娟	杨 硕	杨 曦	杨晓霞	袁 勇
张 静	张 蕾	张 丽	张全生	张新江	张 勇
章新拓	赵江民	郑 颖	周 芳	周 荧	朱 璇
朱 芸					

前言

为帮助“汉语桥—夏/冬令营”学生以及所有对中国感兴趣的外国朋友在较短时间内了解中国的语言与文化、历史与风俗，孔子学院总部/国家汉办组织研发，高等教育出版社于2011年正式出版发行了“中国欢迎你”短期汉语系列教材，受到了海内外教师和学生的普遍认可和喜爱。

为顺应汉语教学与文化体验项目的不断发展，孔子学院总部/国家汉办对教材使用情况开展了调研，编写组由此获得了教师和学生们对教材的宝贵反馈意见，对“中国欢迎你”短期汉语系列教材进行了系统修订和完善，精心研制并推出修订版。

◎ 适用对象

本系列教材主要适用于来华参加夏/冬令营的学生，海外孔子学院和孔子课堂也可将其用作教学辅助资源。

◎ 教材构成

本系列教材分为三大类：语言类、才艺类和地域类。

《学剪纸》是才艺类教材中的一册，主要内容包括对边折剪、连续折剪和多边折剪等不同类型剪纸的折剪方法和图样。本书将文化与才艺学习有机地结合起来，同时配以丰富的练习和活动，目的在于帮助学习者在较短时间内掌握剪纸的基本制作技能。本书的参考教学时间为6～8学时。

◎ 编写特色

1. 适用性：充分考虑海外青少年学习者短期学习的学习特点，以学习者为中心，合理设计教学内容和教学顺序，用深入浅出、图文并茂的方式展示汉语与文化。

2. 活动式：以任务和活动为主线，寓教于乐，注重实效，便于教师进行教学设计，充分调动学习者的学习兴趣，实现轻松有效的课堂教学。

3. 资源性：为教师和学习者提供各类丰富的素材，以及各类可以直接动手操作的练习，满足学习者的个性化需求。

让我们翻开书，一起去感知充满魅力的汉语和中国文化吧！

编委会

2016年2月

Contents 目 录

Chinese Paper-cuts

剪纸

Tools for Making Paper-cuts
剪纸的工具

paper
纸

You can use Chinese red paper or other colored paper.

可以选用中国红纸或其他彩色纸。

scissors
剪刀

Use sharp pointed scissors instead of round pointed scissors.

最好用刀头锋利的尖头剪刀，而不是圆头剪刀。

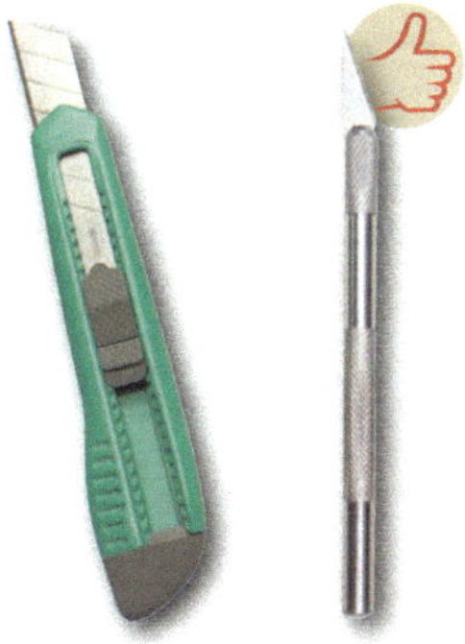

knife
刀

Use a craft knife for cutting designs that you can't manage with scissors.

最好使用刻刀，以便处理那些不便用剪刀剪的图案。

pencil
铅笔

Used for drawing designs.

用来绘制图样。

glue stick
胶棒

Used for sticking finished projects.

用来粘贴完成的作品。

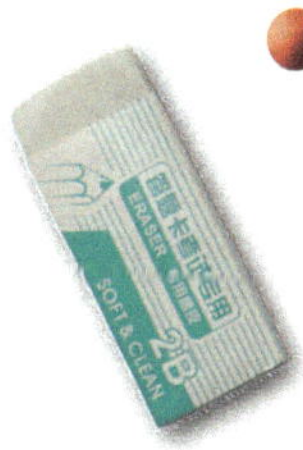

eraser
橡皮

Used for erasing designs.

用来擦改图样。

Single-fold Paper-cuts
对边折剪

Folding Method 折叠方法

Choose an appropriate-sized piece of paper, fold it in half.
根据图形选择尺寸合适的纸，沿中线对折。

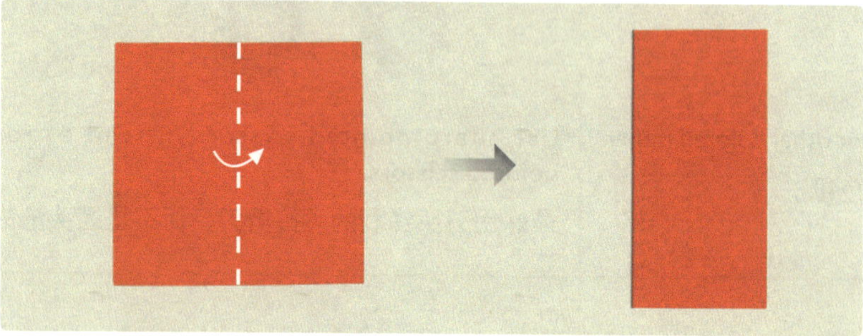

Lattern 灯笼

2-1

dēnglong
灯笼

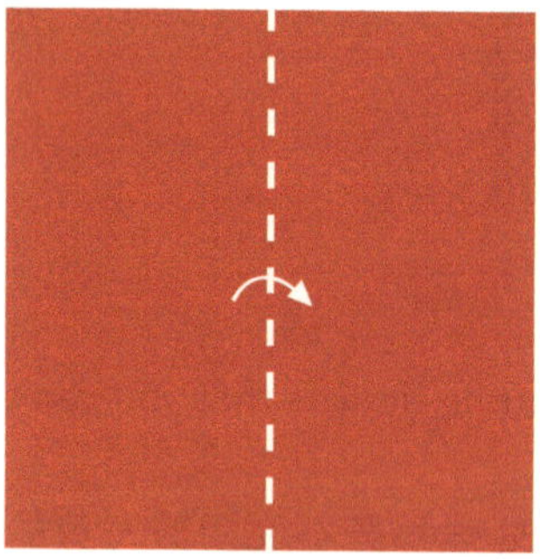

❶ Fold.
折。

❷ Draw.
画。

❸ Cut.
剪。

❹ Unfold and complete.
展开，完成。

Goldfish 金鱼

3-2

jīnyú

金鱼

Butterfly 蝴蝶

3-3

húdié

蝴蝶

“Spring” (Chinese character) 春

4-4

chūn

春

Panda 熊猫

4-5

xióngmāo

熊猫

Let's Try 试一试

You can stick your panda paper-cut to this page!

将你的熊猫剪纸作品贴在本页吧！

Let's Think 想一想

What can be found in the paper-cut below? Put a tick below the corresponding pictures.

下面的剪纸作品中包含哪些元素？在相应的图片下边画 ✓。

1

2

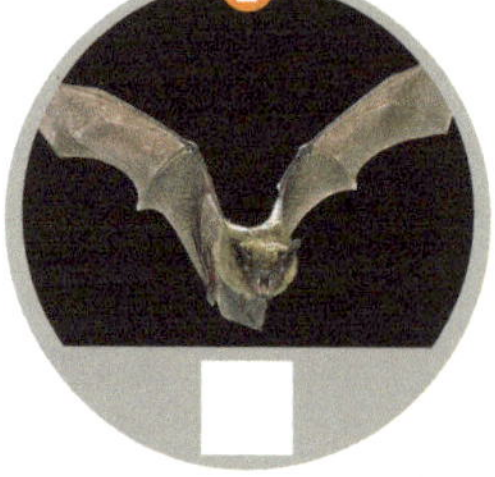

3

4

5

6

7

8

Chain-fold Paper-cuts
连续折剪

Folding Method A 折叠方法A

1. Fold the paper according to the instructions below.
按照指示折纸。

2. Draw your design on the side highlighted in the design below.
在如图所示的一面画图样。

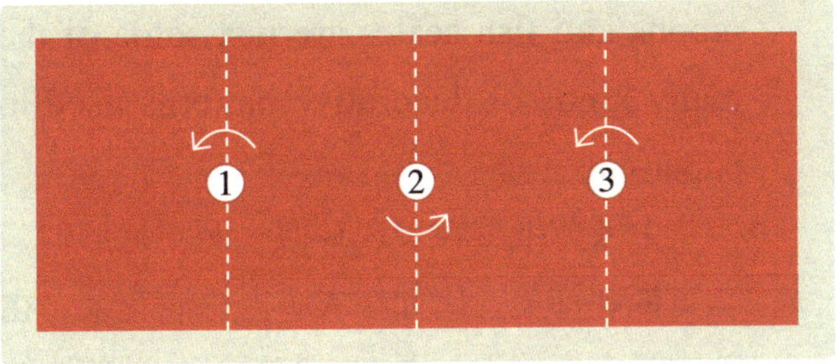

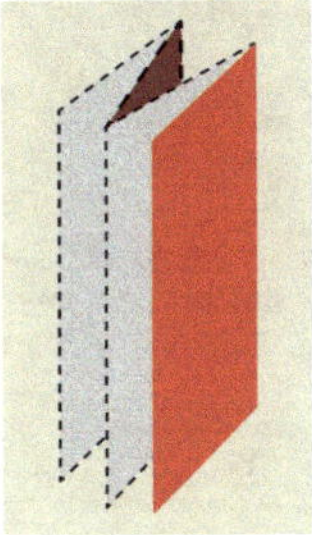

Fold outwards.
纸往外折。
Fold inwards.
纸往里折。

"Happiness" (Chinese character) 囍

If you ever have the opportunity to attend a Chinese wedding, you will probably find the Chinese character "囍" everywhere you look: pasted on doors, on windows, on walls and on the wedding cars. This is an important part of traditional Chinese weddings.

贴"囍"字是中国婚俗文化中的一项重要内容。如果你能有机会参加中国人的婚礼，你会发现，门上、窗户上、墙壁上、婚车上——到处都贴着红色的"囍"字。

7-1

xǐ
囍
happiness

Chinese paper-cuts do not usually bear a close resemblance to the objects they represent, instead focusing on capturing the essence or spirit of the object, with a great deal of emphasis also placed on ornate decoration, such as covering a dress with flowers, or drawing patterns on the bodies of animal designs. Saw-teeth, crescent moons and fish scales are just some of the many kinds of decorative patterns used in paper-cuts.

中国剪纸重在表现神似，而不是形似。它重视装饰美，比如在衣服上缀满花朵，在动物身上直接添加图案。剪纸有各种装饰纹样，比如锯齿形、月牙形、鱼鳞形都是常用的剪纸图案。

Folding Method B 折叠方法B

❶ Fold the paper according to the instructions below.
按照指示折纸。

❷ Draw your design on the side highlighted in the design below.
在如图所示的一面画图样。

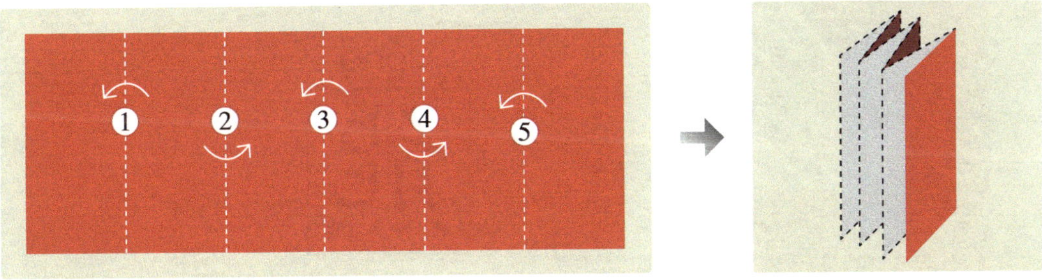

Tips 小贴士

If you draw a complete design on one side, you only need to fold two V shapes in order to get a chain of four pictures.

图样是完整图案时，要剪出四个完整的图形图，就应该折叠出两个V形。

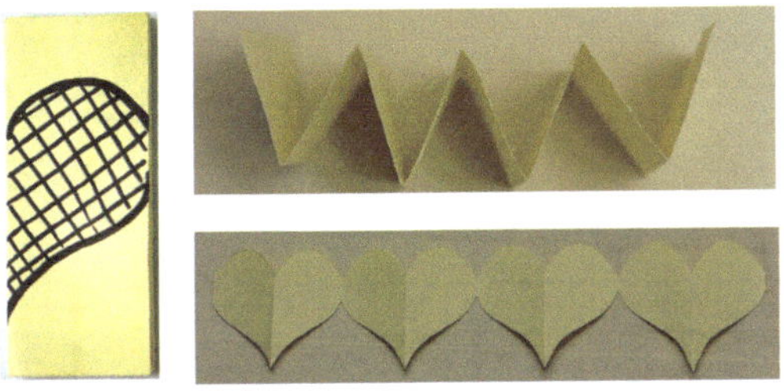

If you draw only half the design on one side, you will need to fold four V shapes in order to cut out a chain of four complete pictures.

图样是半幅图案时，要剪出四个完整的图形，就应该折叠出四个V形。

If you draw a half-design, make sure it is adjacent to the folded edge of the paper.

最好将图案画在靠近折痕的一边。

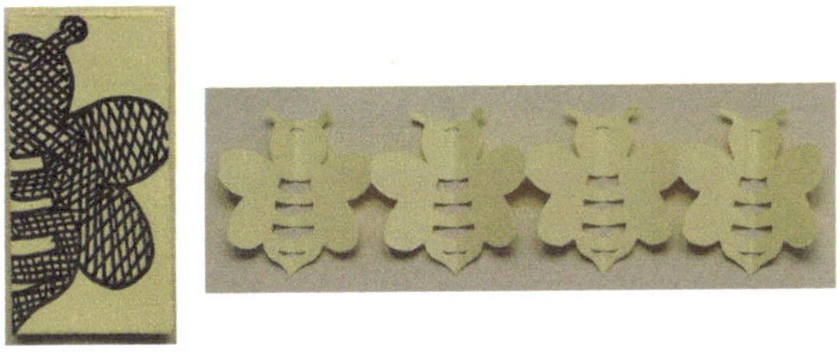

The designs from single-fold paper-cuts can all be used to make chain-fold paper-cuts. The key is to make sure both sides remain connected.

对边折剪的图案都可以用到连续折剪中来，要点就是保证两边不剪断。

Bear 熊

Designs must be drawn to touch both sides of the paper.
一定要贴着纸的左右两边画图样。

xióng

熊

Chrysanthemum Flower 菊花

júhuā

菊花

Let's Try 试一试

Work in pairs and try to cut out the designs on the right. See which pair finishes first and whose paper-cut is the best.

两人一组，试试看能不能剪出右边的图案，并将剪好的作品贴在下面。比一比哪个组完成得又快又好。

Multi-edged Paper-cuts
多边折剪

Folding Method A 折叠方法A

Select a square piece of paper, fold it in half diagonally along the dashed lines.
选择一张正方形的纸，沿线折叠。

12-1

13-2

13-3

Folding Method B 折叠方法B

1. Select a square piece of paper, fold it in half diagonally along the dashed line.
选择正方形的纸，沿线对折。

2. Measure the angles as shown.
找好角度。

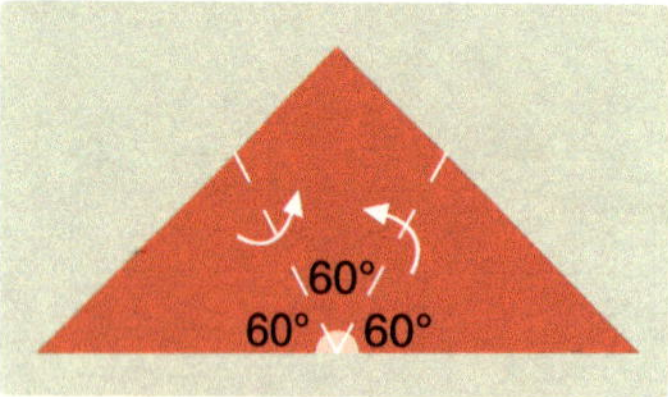

3. Fold it along the dashed lines.
沿线折叠。

15-5

15-6

Folding Method C 折叠方法C

1. Select a square piece of paper, fold it in half once diagonally.
选择正方形的纸，沿线对折一次。

2. Measure the angles as shown.
找好角度。

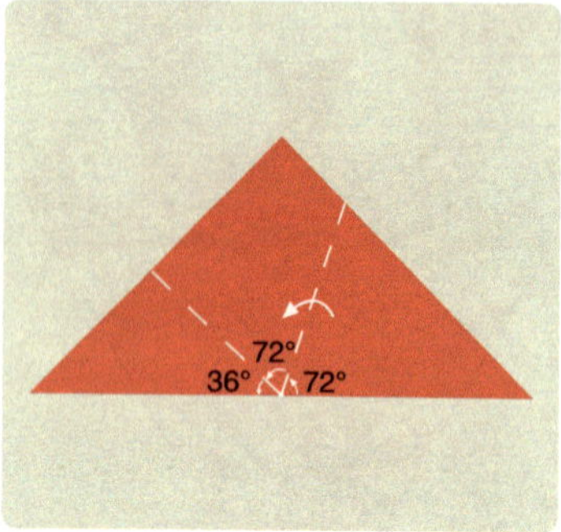

3. Fold it along the dashed lines.
沿线折叠。

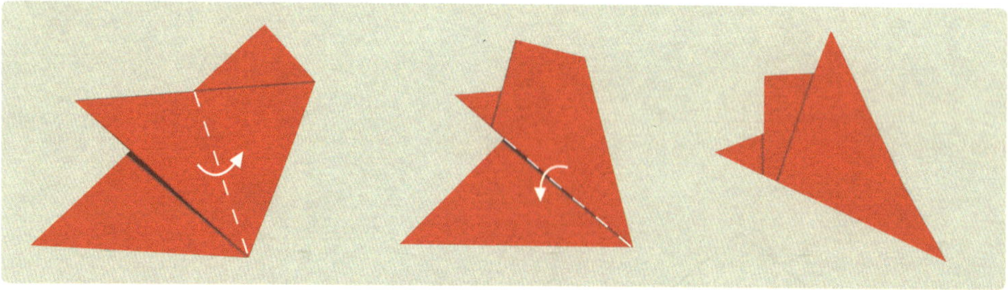

16-7

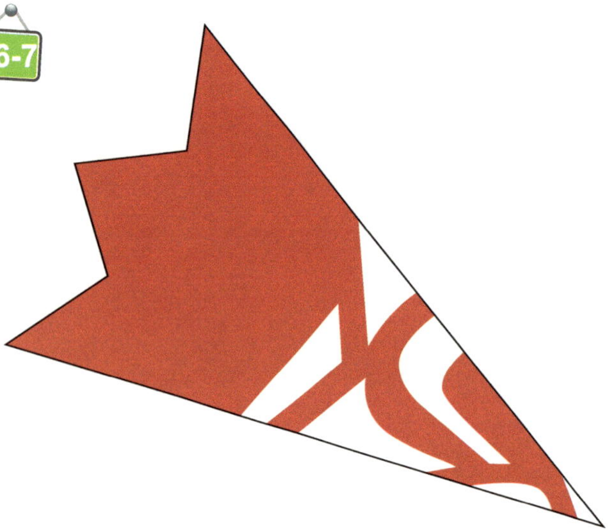

17-8

17-9

Let's Try 试一试

Now that you've learned various different ways to fold the paper, try designing new patterns and creating your own paper-cuts.

掌握了各种折叠方法之后，你也可以试着自己设计图样，创作独一无二的剪纸作品。

Paper-cuts Designs and Materials
剪纸图样与素材

Fold outwards.
纸往外折。
Fold inwards.
纸往里折。

2-1

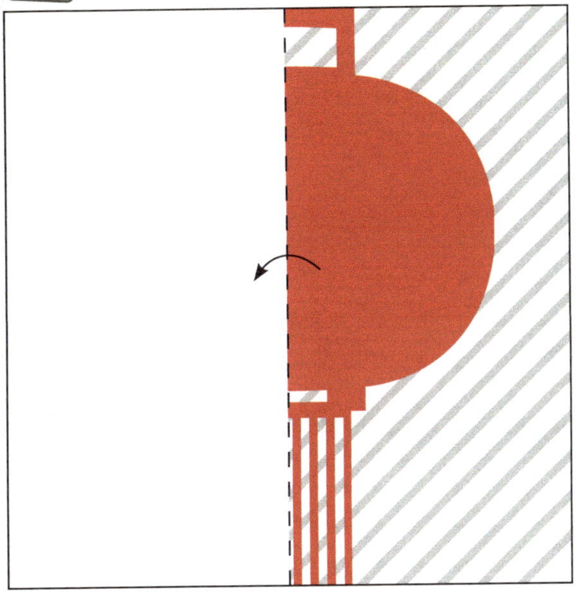

3-2

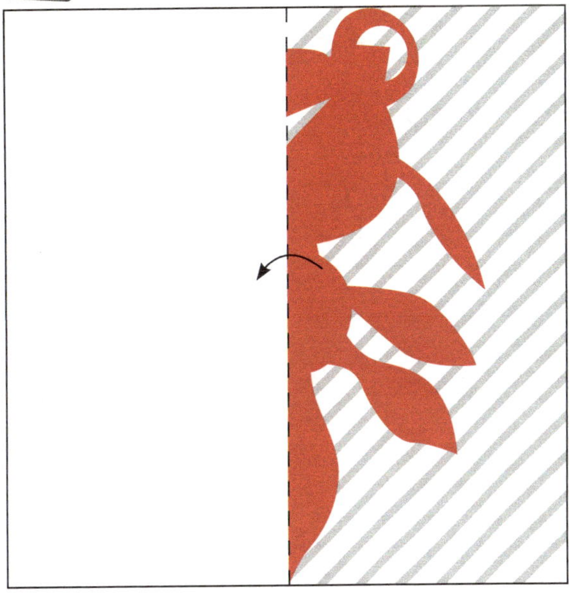

3-3

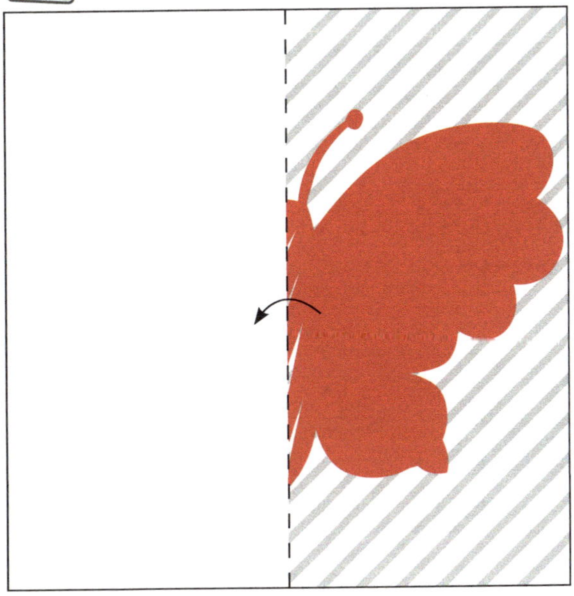

4-4

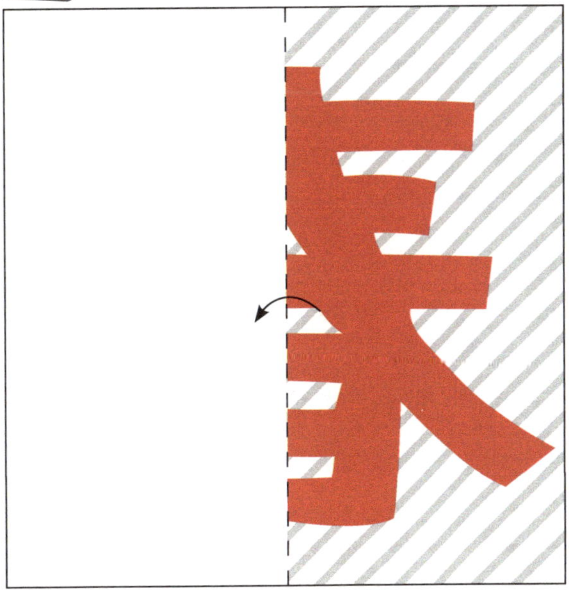

4-5

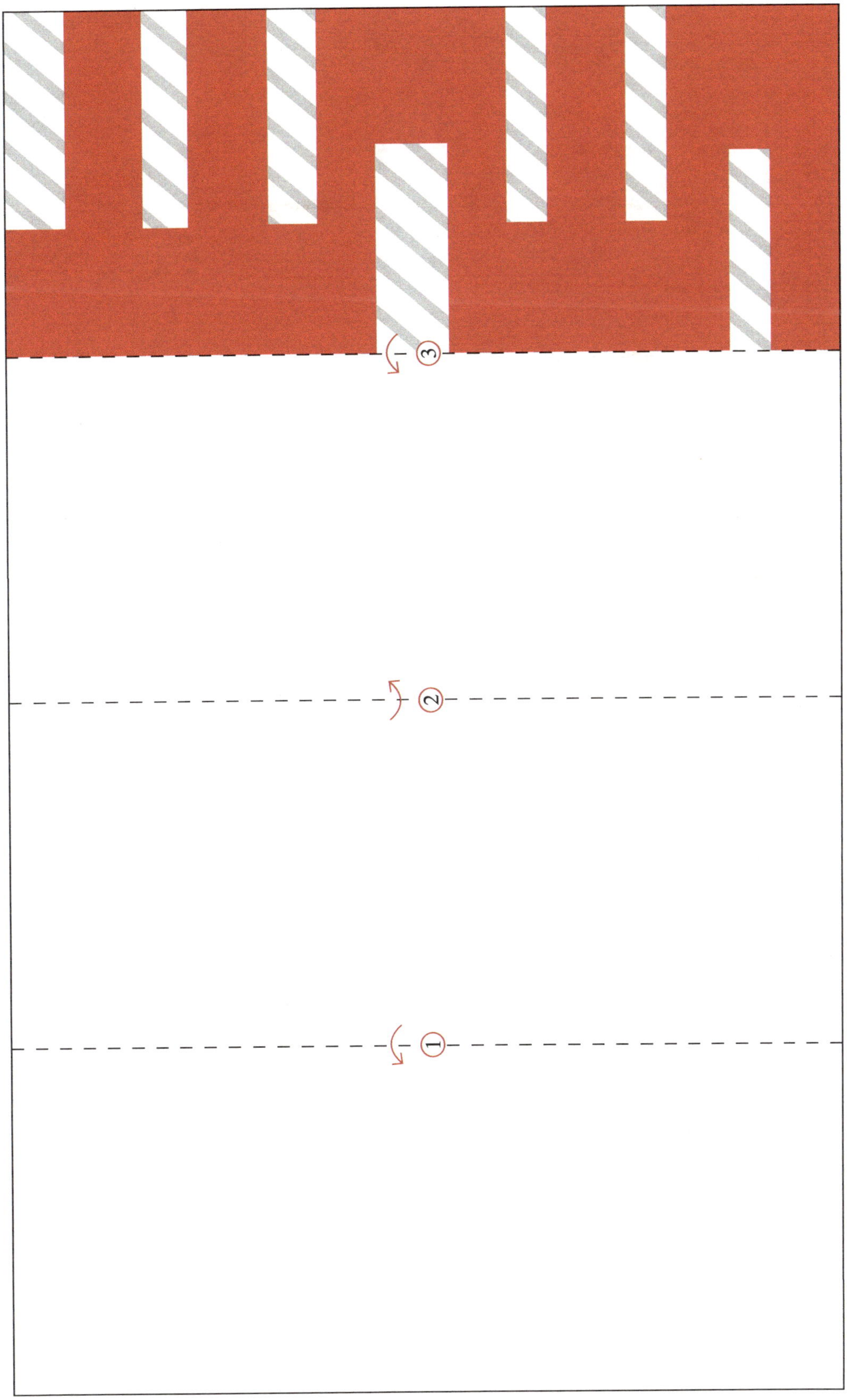

7-1

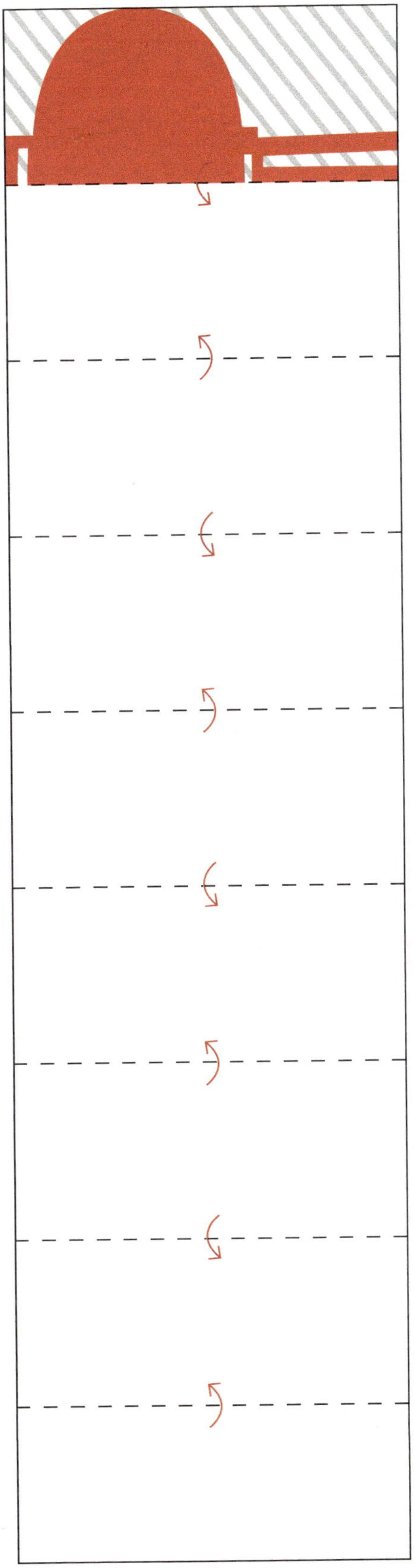

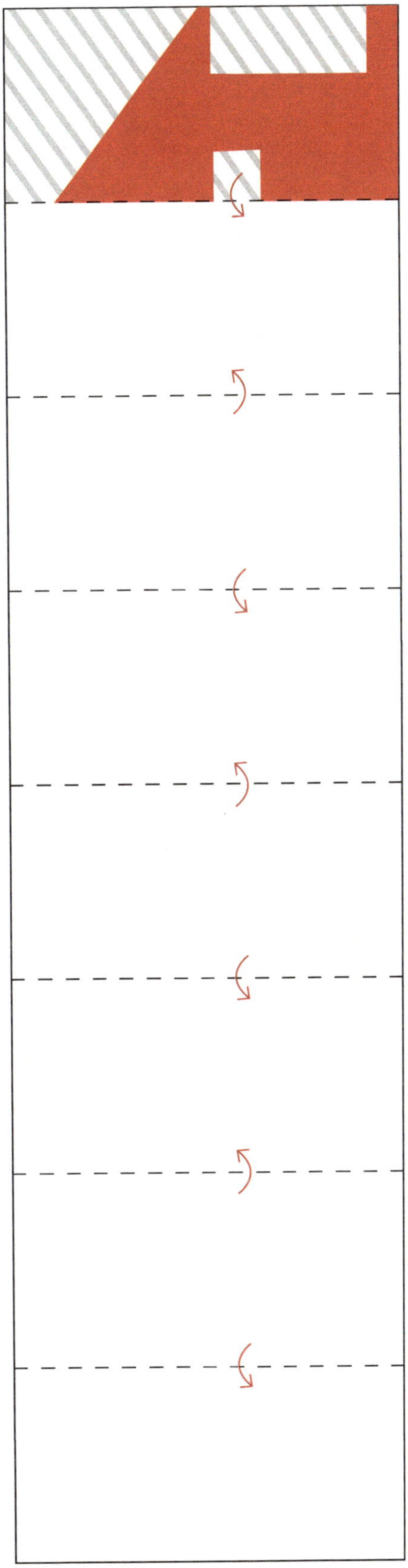

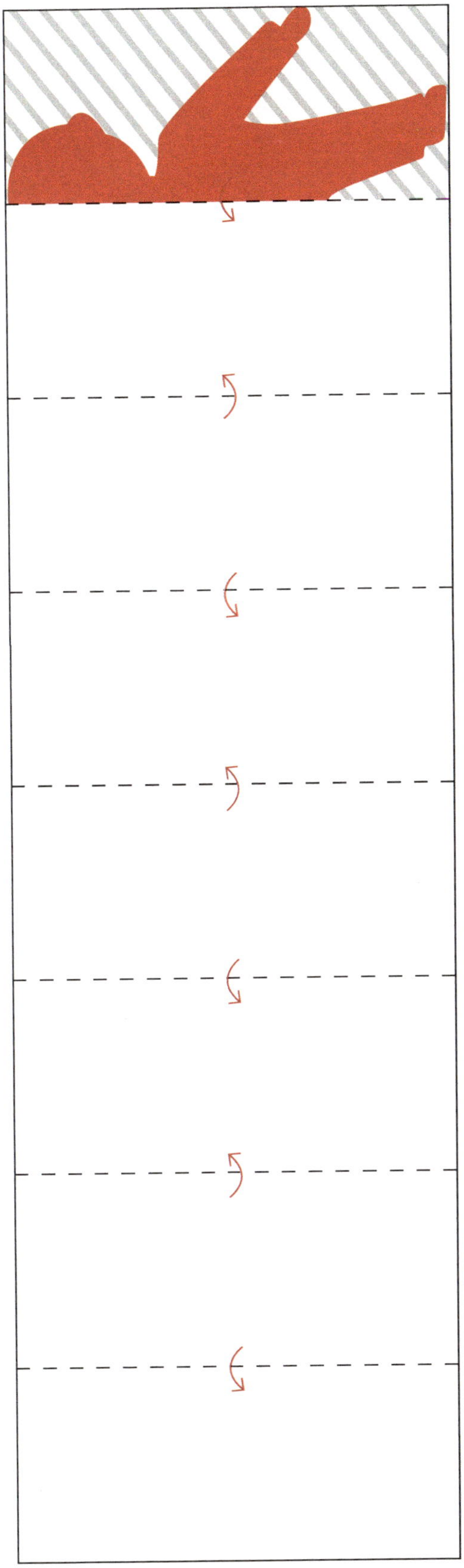

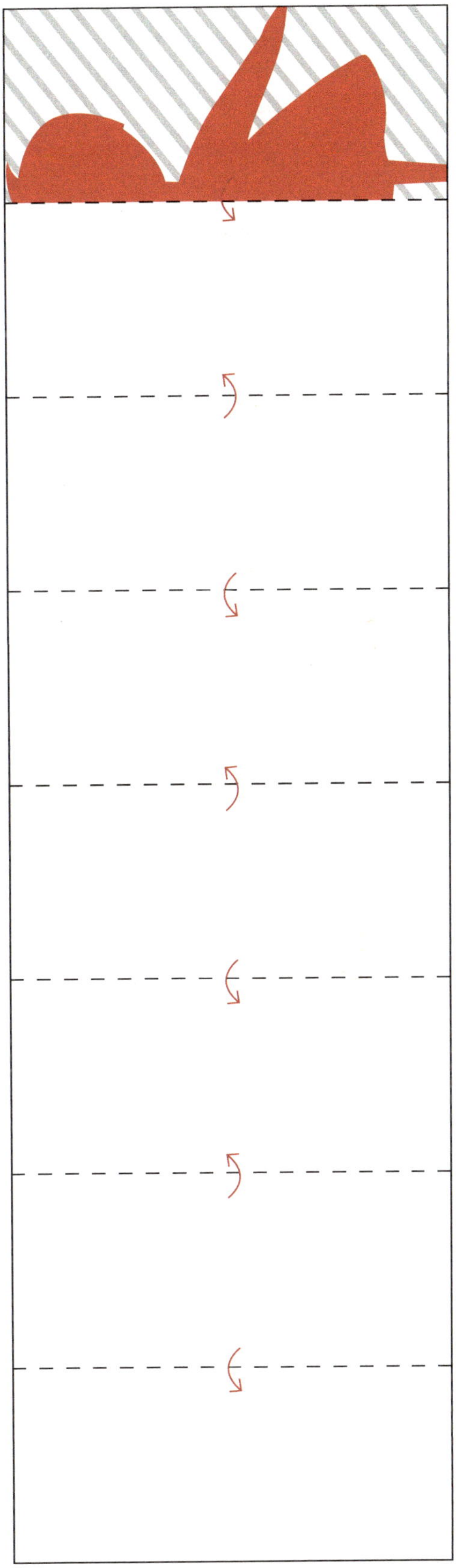

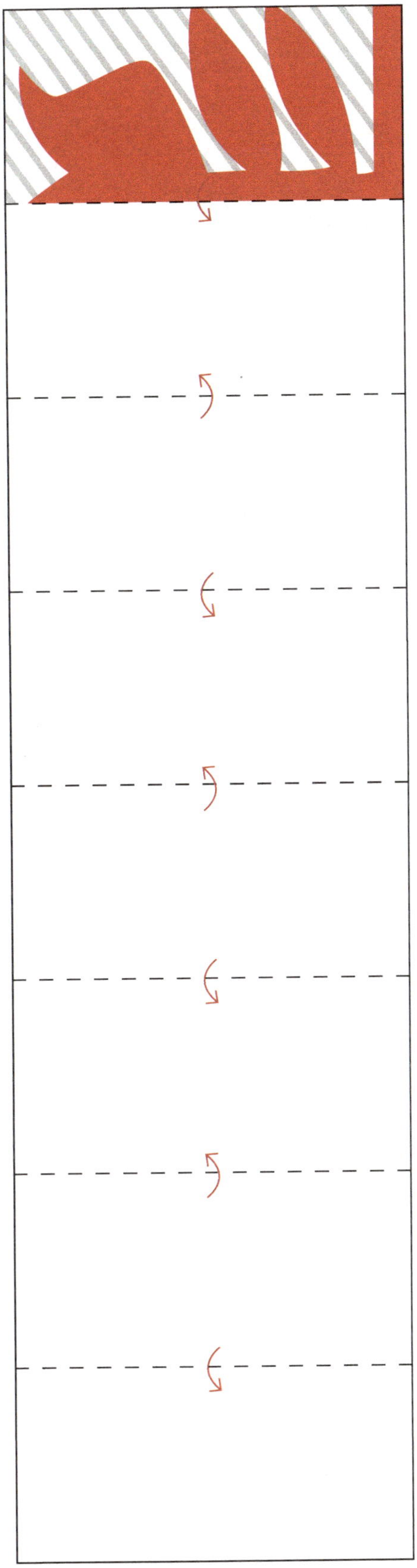

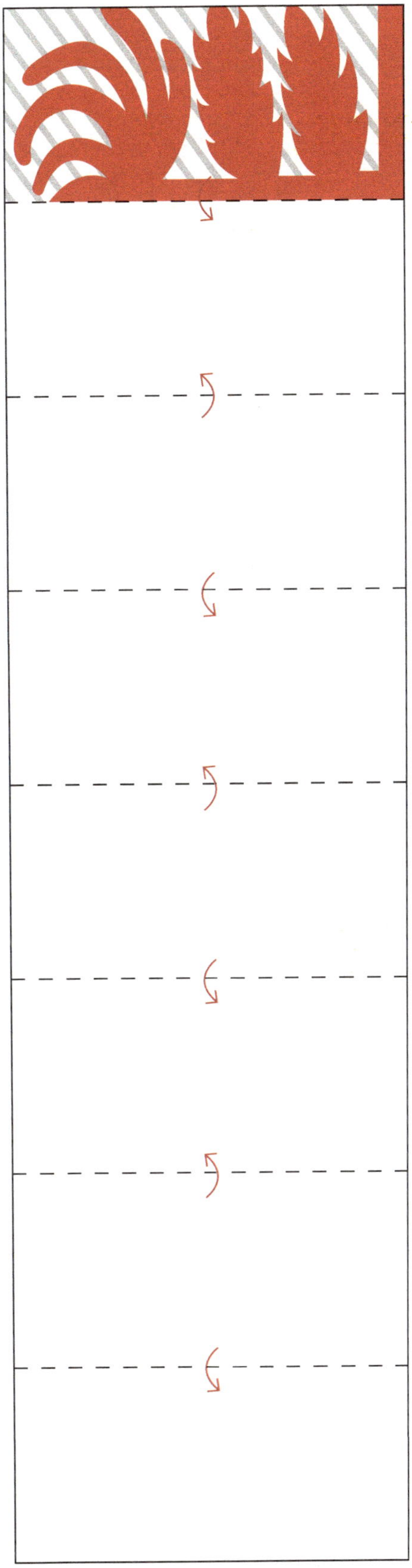

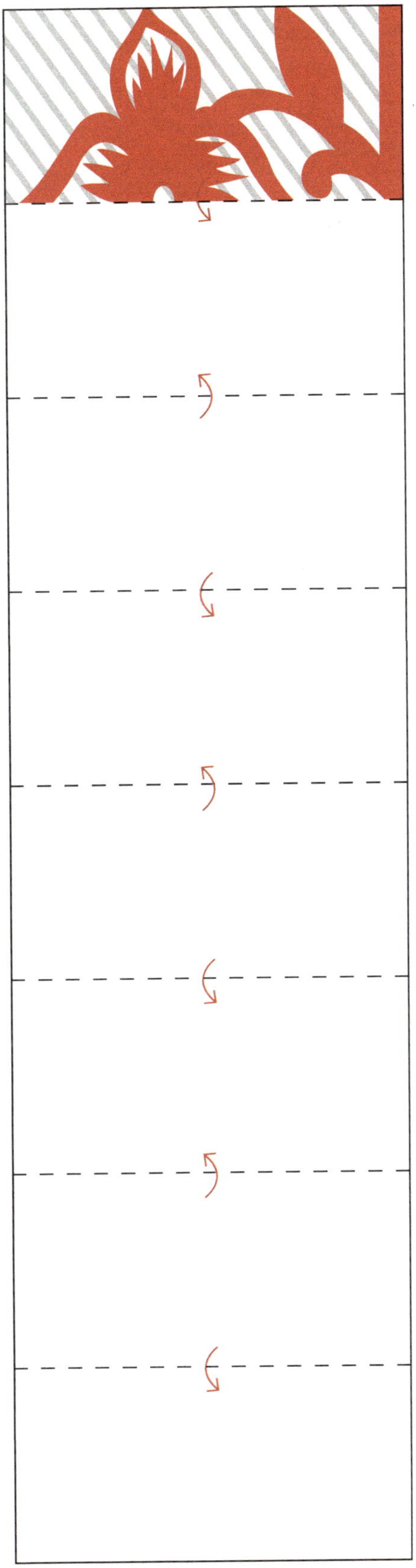

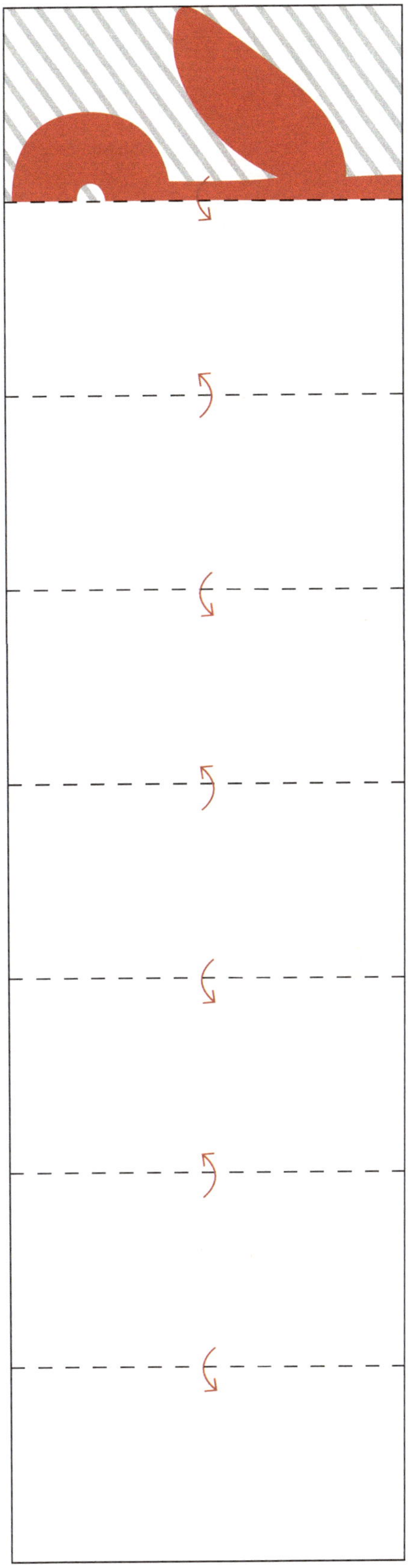

12-1

13-2

13-3

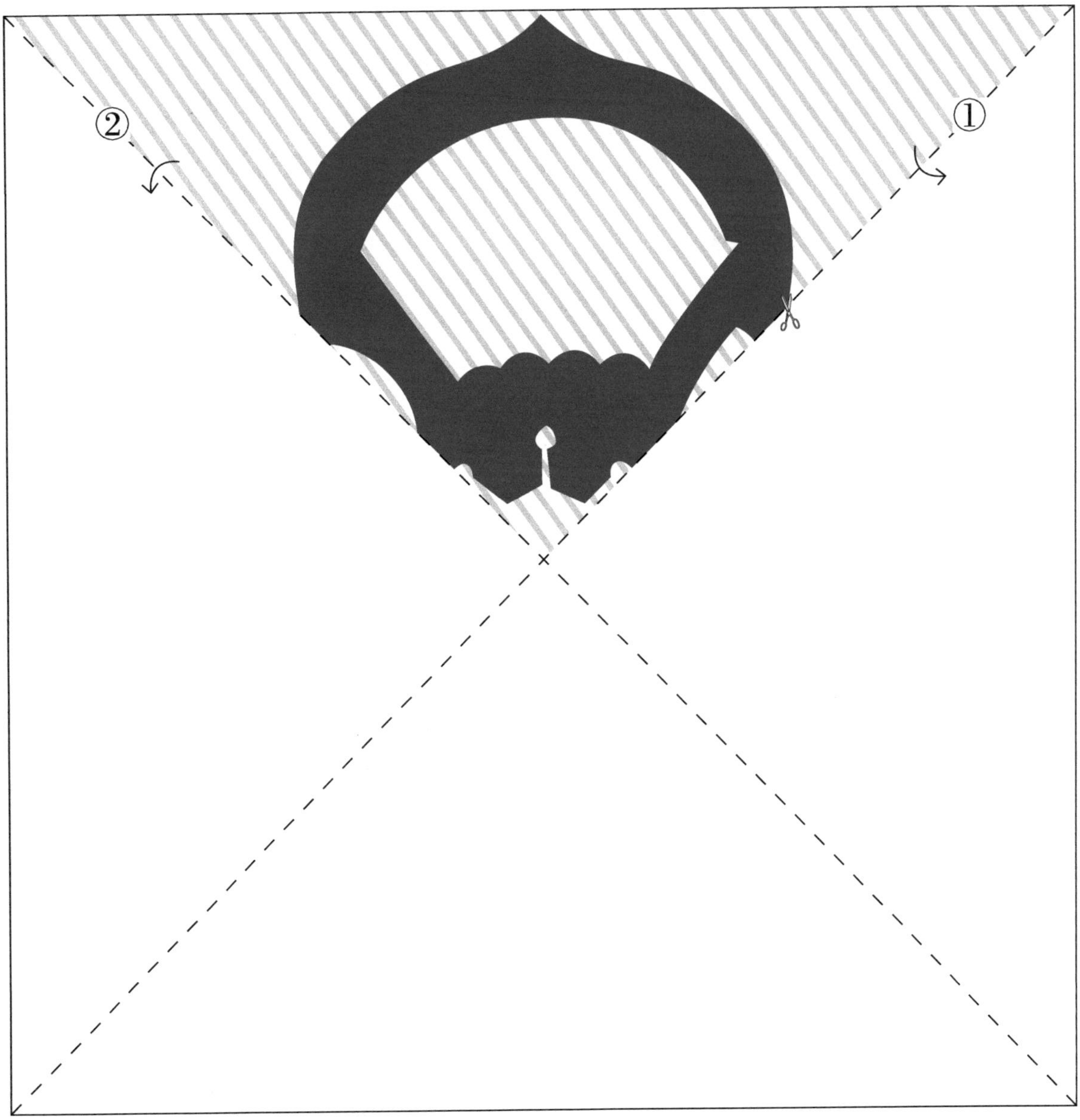

14-4

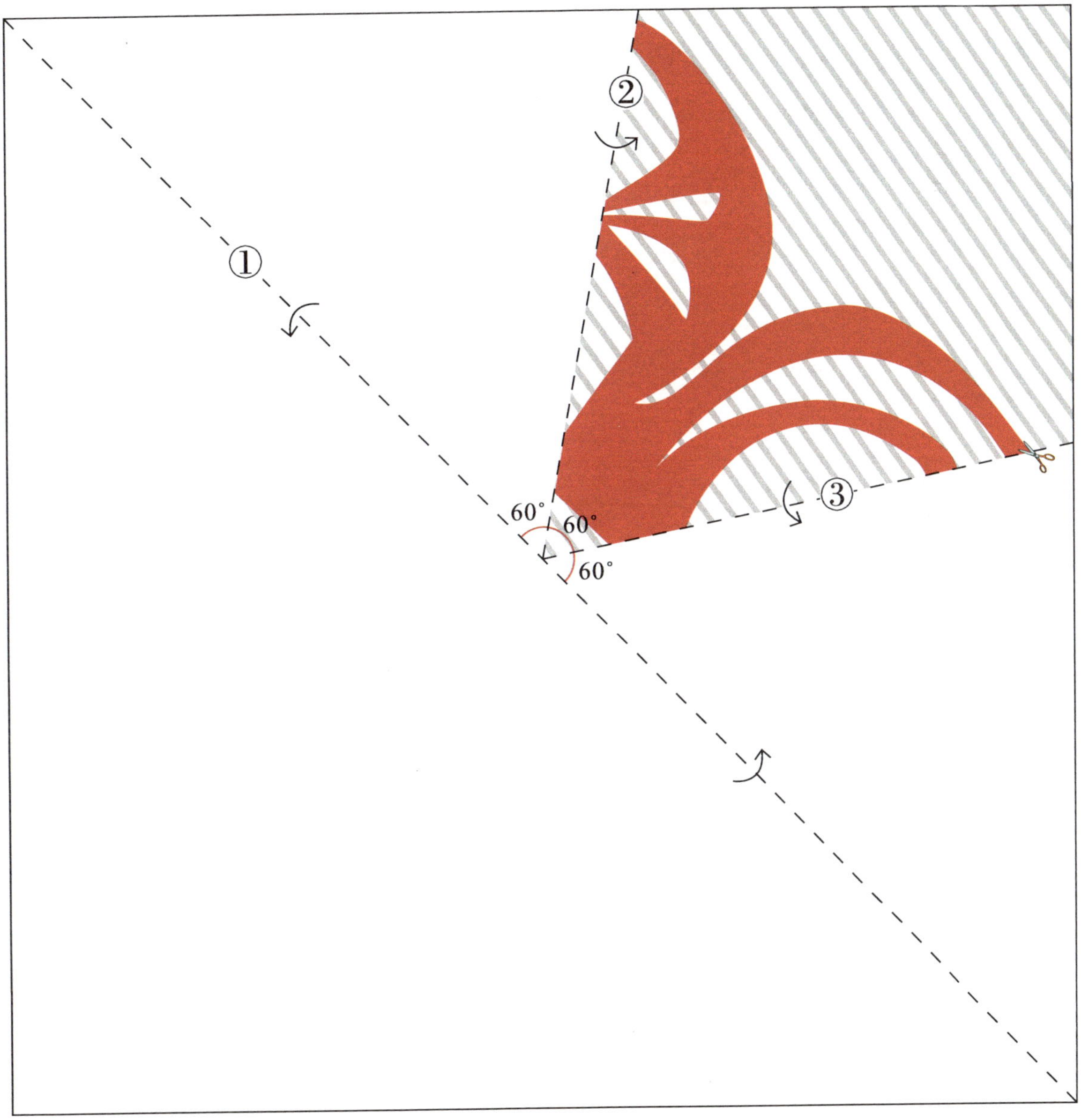

15-5

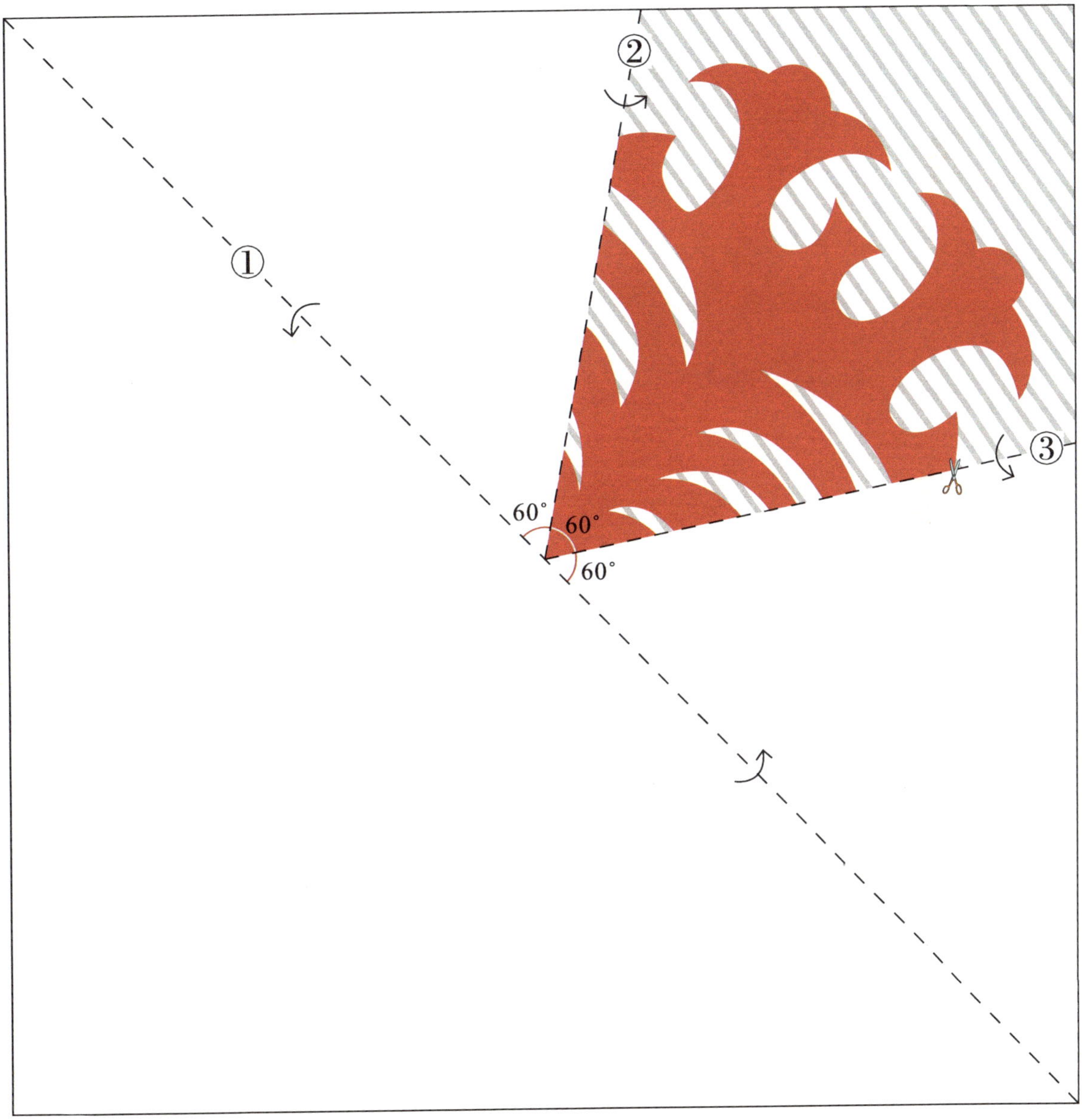

15-6

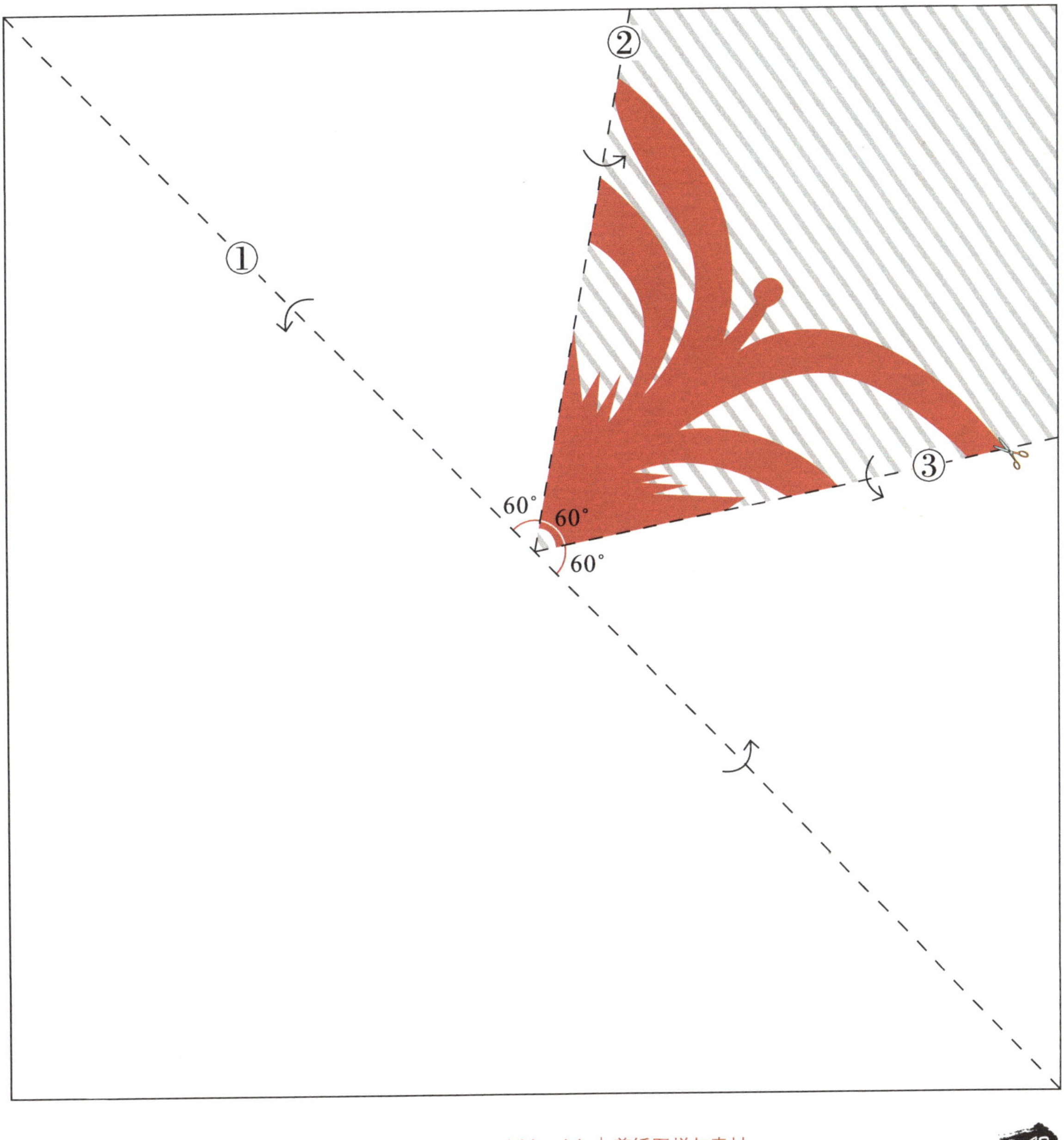

16-7

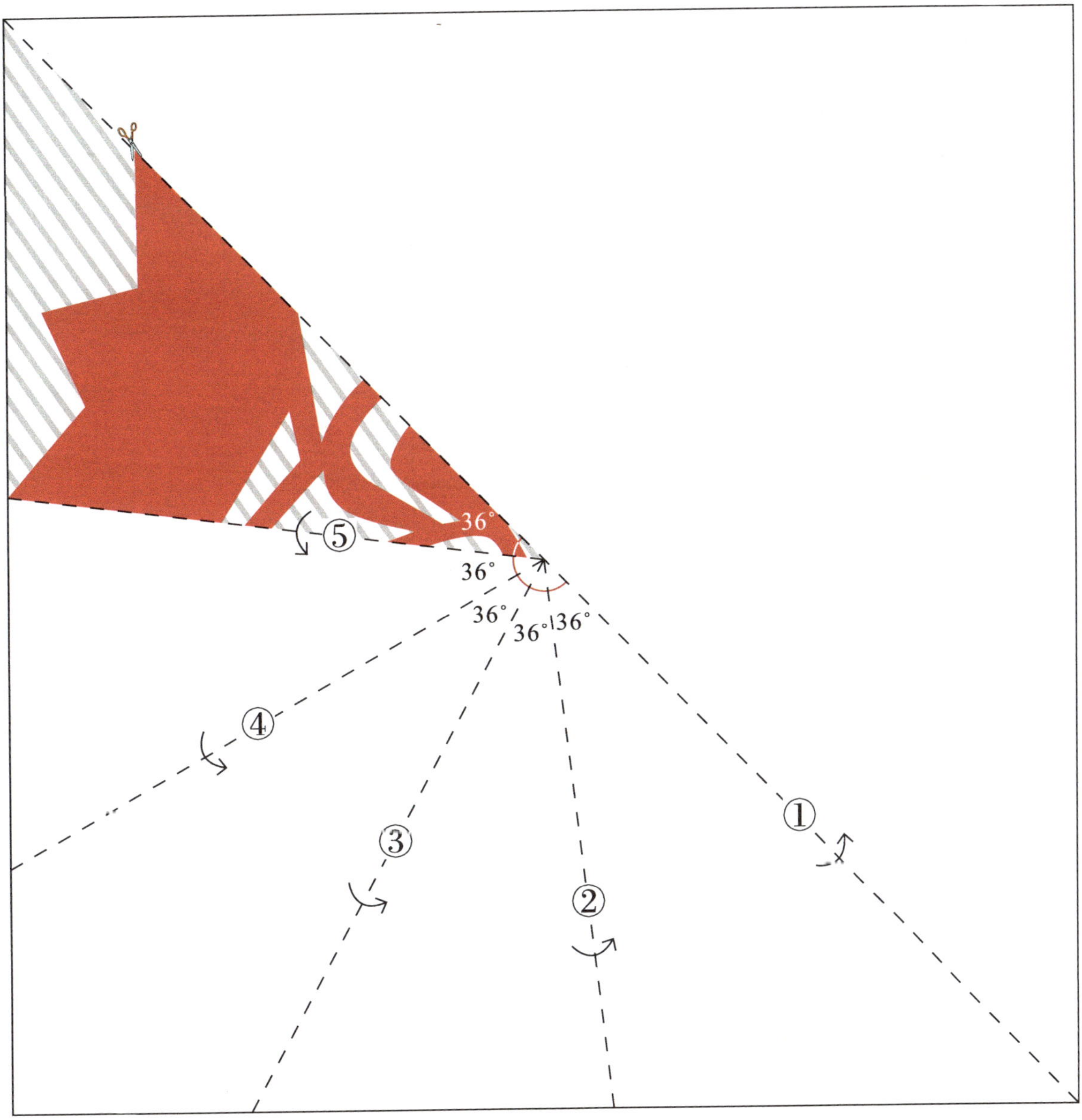

17-8

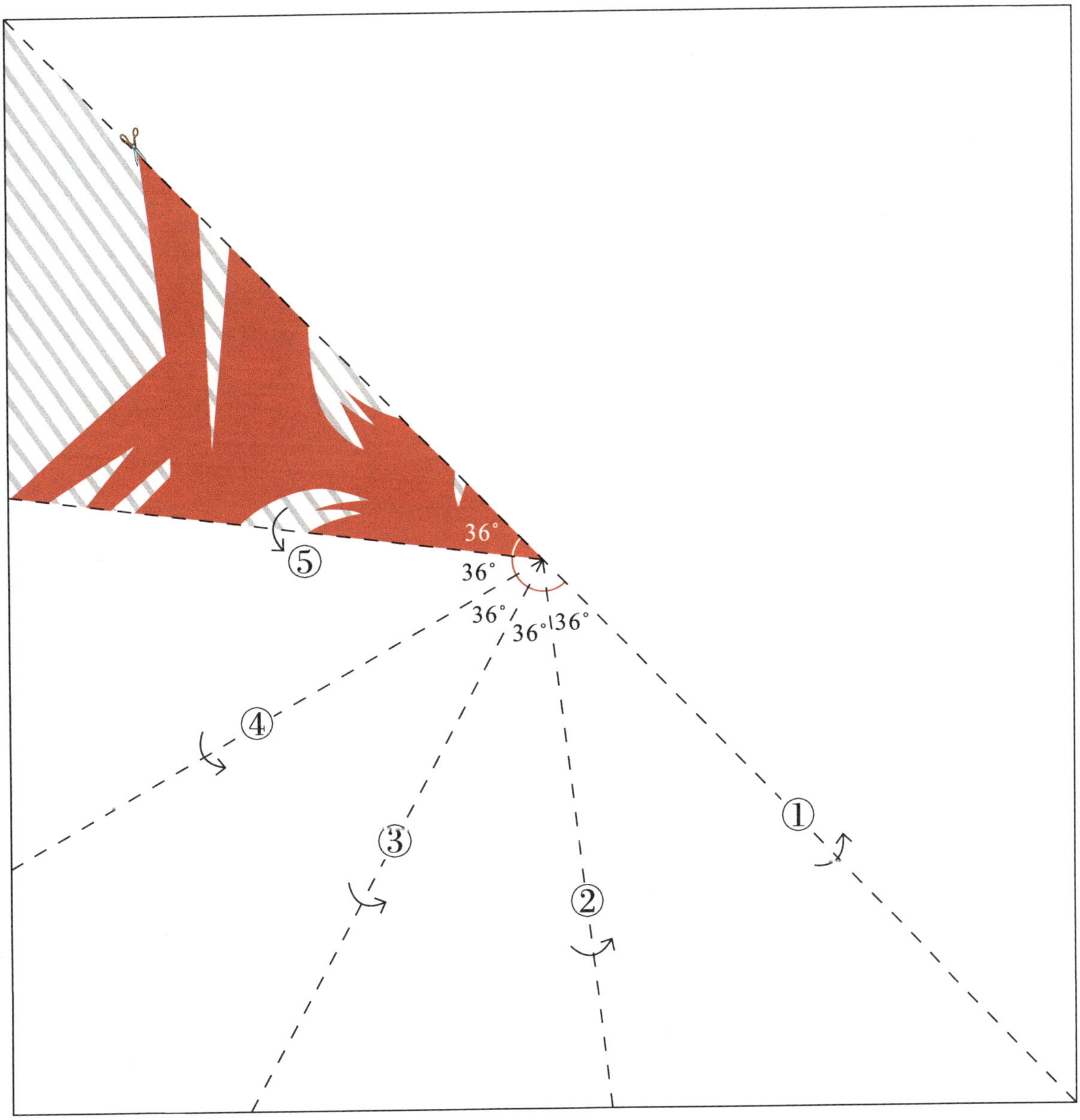

17-9

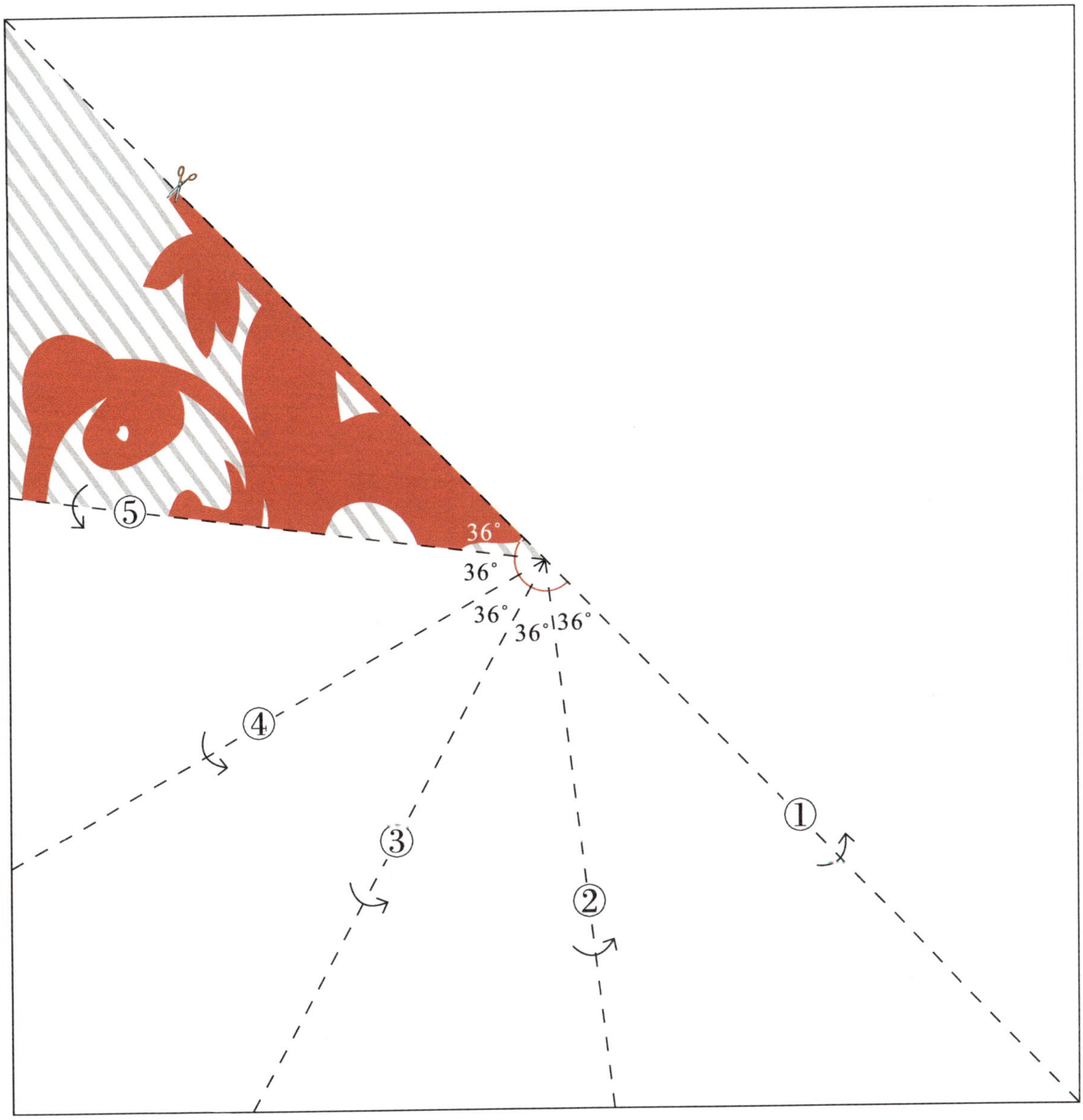

郑重声明

高等教育出版社依法对本书享有专有出版权。任何未经许可的复制、销售行为均违反《中华人民共和国著作权法》，其行为人将承担相应的民事责任和行政责任；构成犯罪的，将被依法追究刑事责任。为了维护市场秩序，保护读者的合法权益，避免读者误用盗版书造成不良后果，我社将配合行政执法部门和司法机关对违法犯罪的单位和个人进行严厉打击。社会各界人士如发现上述侵权行为，希望及时举报，我社将奖励举报有功人员。

反盗版举报电话　(010) 58581999　58582371

反盗版举报邮箱　dd@hep.com.cn

通信地址　北京市西城区德外大街4号　高等教育出版社法律事务部

邮政编码　100120

读者意见反馈

为收集对教材的意见建议，进一步完善教材编写并做好服务工作，读者可将对本教材的意见建议通过如下渠道反馈至我社。

咨询电话　400-810-0598

反馈邮箱　wy_dzyj@pub.hep.cn

通信地址　北京市朝阳区惠新东街4号富盛大厦1座
　　　　　高等教育出版社总编辑办公室

邮政编码　100029

图书在版编目（CIP）数据

中国欢迎你．学剪纸 / 孔子学院总部 / 国家汉办编著．-- 2版（修订本）．-- 北京：高等教育出版社，2016.6（2023.9重印）
“中国欢迎你”短期汉语系列教材
ISBN 978-7-04-044981-5

Ⅰ．①中… Ⅱ．①孔… Ⅲ．①汉语－对外汉语教学－教材 Ⅳ．①H195.4

中国版本图书馆CIP数据核字（2016）第074050号

策划编辑 鞠 慧　责任编辑 鞠 慧 杨 曦　剪纸创作 李 桑 王业霞 杨 曦　封面设计 乔 剑
版式设计 三月天地　英文审译 Simon Golding　插图选配 杨 曦　责任校对 杨 曦
责任印制 耿 轩

出版发行 高等教育出版社
社　　址 北京市西城区德外大街4号
邮政编码 100120
印　　刷 河北信瑞彩印刷有限公司
开　　本 787 mm× 1092 mm 1/16
印　　张 3.5
字　　数 87千字
购书热线 010-58581118
咨询电话 400-810-0598
网　　址 http://www.hep.edu.cn
　　　　 http://www.hep.com.cn
网上订购 http://www.hepmall.com.cn
　　　　 http://www.hepmall.com
　　　　 http://www.hepmall.cn
版　　次 2011年6月第1版
　　　　 2016年6月第2版
印　　次 2023年9月第6次印刷
定　　价 16.80元

本书如有缺页、倒页、脱页等质量问题，请到所购图书销售部门联系调换
版权所有 侵权必究
物 料 号 44981-00